HAL LEONARD

DRUMS FOR KIDS

A Beginner's Guide with Step-by-Step Instruction for Drumset

To access audio visit:
www.halleonard.com/mylibrary

Enter Code
8803-4708-4710-8968

Drumset for photos provided by Yamaha.

ISBN 978-1-4803-0223-5

HAL•LEONARD® CORPORATION
7777 W. BLUEMOUND RD. P.O. BOX 13819 MILWAUKEE, WI 53213

Visit Hal Leonard Online at
www.halleonard.com

SETTING UP YOUR DRUMSET

Take a look at the drumset below and the names of each piece. Start by setting up your drums like this. You may then adjust each piece so that it's comfortable and easy for you to reach.

Start by adjusting the height of your stool. When sitting on it, you should look like this:

When sitting on the stool with your feet on the bass drum and hi-hat pedals, the snare drum should be between your legs. Adjust the height of the snare drum so the top is a little higher than your knees.

Adjust the tom-toms and cymbals so everything is within reach like this:

HOW TO HOLD YOUR STICKS

Drumsticks come in many sizes. Start out by trying a few different sizes to feel what works best for you. Choosing good quality drumsticks is important for even weight and balance. Some good general sizes to start with are 7a, 5a, and 5b.

Tip   Shoulder   Shaft   Butt

Let's start by learning to hold the sticks with **matched grip**. Begin by holding one stick in your right hand with your thumb and index finger to create a pivot point like this:

Your other fingers should grip the stick, but wrap around loosely. Don't hold it all the way at the back of the stick, but rather leave a couple inches like this:

Now hold the other stick the same way with your left hand.

HOW TO READ MUSIC

Music is written with notes and rests. A **note** means to play; a **rest** means to rest (or pause).

All notes and rests are written on a **staff**, which consists of five lines and four spaces. For drummers, each line and space represents a different drum or cymbal on the drumset. A symbol on the left side of the staff called a **percussion clef** tells you this is a staff for drums. Take a look below to see if you can identify where your different drums and cymbals are on the staff.

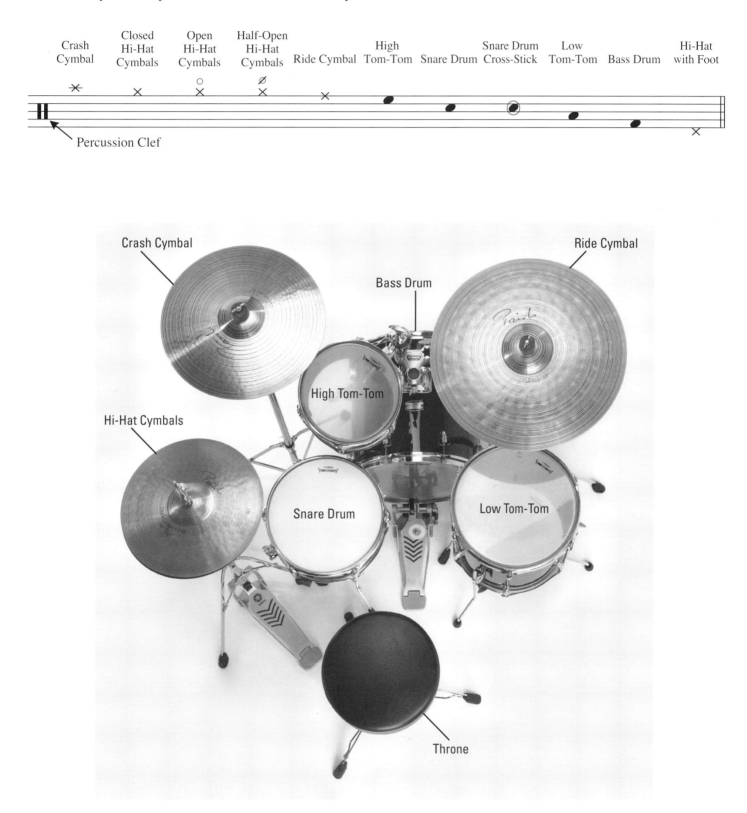

NOTES AND RESTS

Every note or rest has a rhythmic value. This tells you how long, or for how many **beats**, it will last:

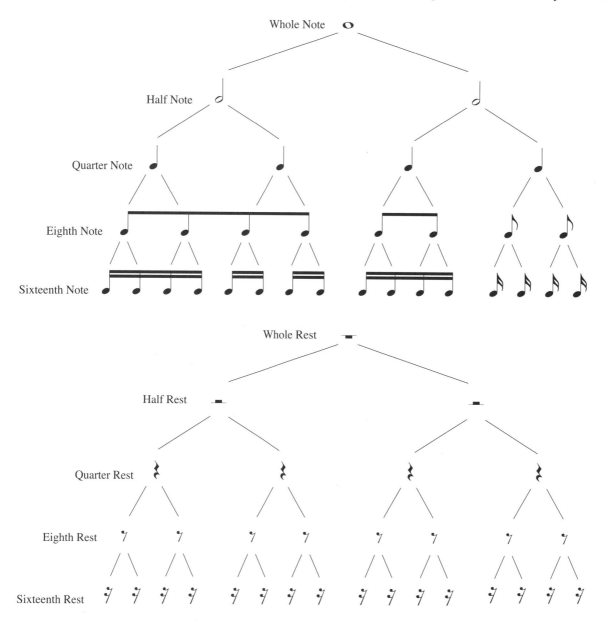

TIME SIGNATURES

Bar lines on the staff separate notes into measures. A **measure** is the space between bar lines. A **double bar line** (thin and thick) shows the end of a piece of music.

There are two numbers that appear at the beginning of a piece of music called a **time signature**. The top number tells how many beats are in each measure and the bottom number tells what kind of note gets one beat. In 4/4 (four-four) time, there are four beats in each measure and the **quarter note** gets one beat.

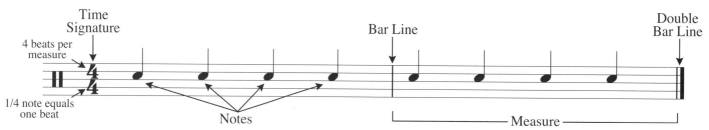

THE SNARE DRUM

Snare drum notes are written on the third space up from the bottom on the staff.

Sometimes snare drum music may have an "R" or "L" above or beneath the notes indicating to play with your right or left stick. Let's begin by playing quarter notes on the snare drum. Hit the center of the snare drum with your sticks in this position:

Count "1, 2, 3, 4, 1, 2, 3, 4…" out loud as you play.

LET'S PLAY!

For each type of note there is also the same kind of rest. A rest means to play nothing during that time. A **quarter rest** looks like this: ♩, and is worth one beat, just like the quarter note, but you simply play nothing for one beat, or count.

QUARTER NOTES AND QUARTER RESTS

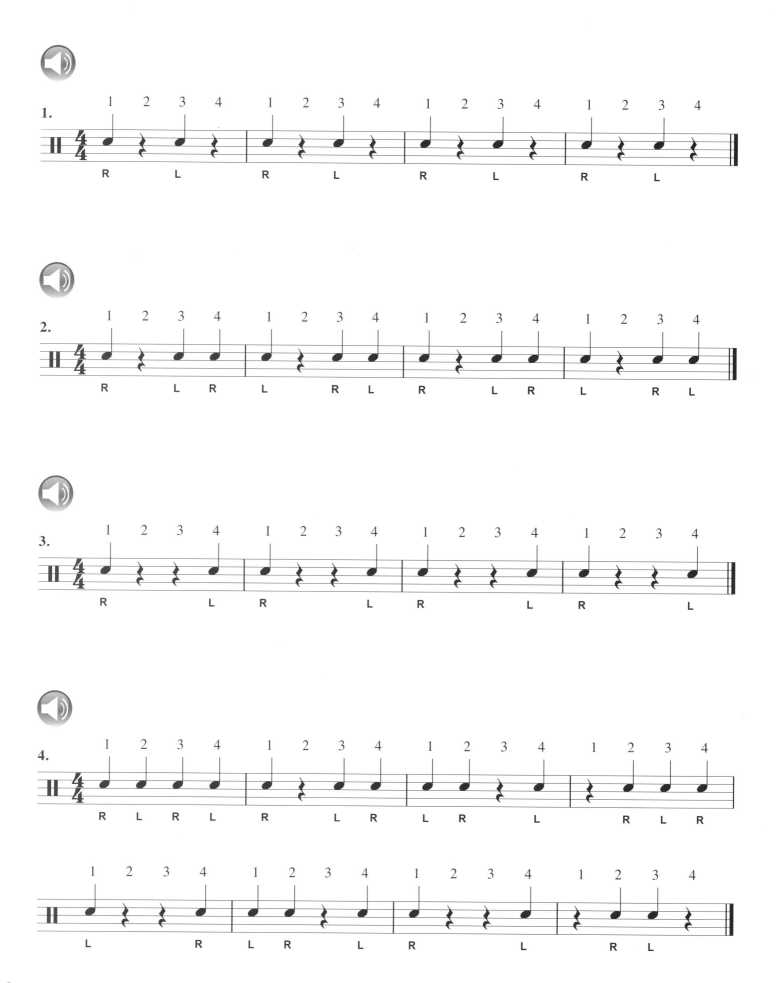

Eighth notes look just like quarter notes but with a **flag** added to the **stem**. If there are two or more eighth notes, they are joined together with a **beam** instead of a flag.

Eighth notes are twice as fast as quarter notes (two eighths equal one quarter note), and are counted "1 and 2 and 3 and 4 and." Let's try some eighth notes now.

EIGHTH NOTES

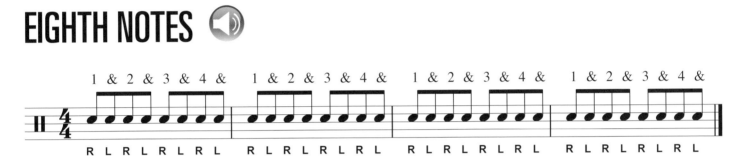

Now combine quarter notes, eighth notes, and quarter rests for the following examples.

QUARTER NOTES, EIGHTH NOTES, QUARTER RESTS

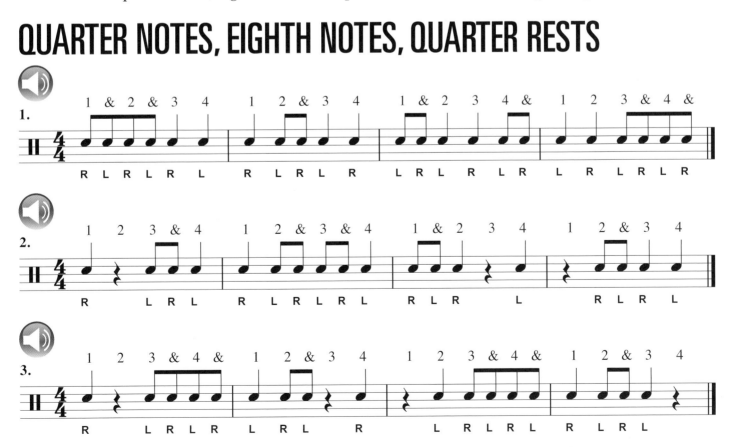

An **eighth rest** looks like this: ⁊, and is worth a half beat just like an eighth note, only you play nothing during the rest.

EIGHTH RESTS

Now let's try everything you know so far. Always remember: a drummer's most important job is keeping a steady, even beat.

PUT IT TOGETHER

THE BASS DRUM

The **bass drum** (or **kick drum**) is played with a pedal using your right foot. It can be played two different ways: heel down with the foot flat pressing the pedal, or heel up using just the ball of the foot to press the pedal. Try both and decide what works best for you.

Bass drum notes are on the bottom space of the staff with the stem facing down.

MY RIGHT FOOT

1.

2.

Now combine the snare drum and bass drum together. Play all of the snare drum notes with your left stick. Take it slow at first, then play at a faster **tempo** (speed) when you're ready.

PURPLE HAZE

Words and Music by
Jimi Hendrix

THE RIDE CYMBAL

The **ride cymbal** is the largest cymbal located on your right side when seated behind your drums. It's usually played with the tip of the right stick on the surface of the cymbal.

TAKE A RIDE

Now try playing this song with the ride, snare, and bass drum. Play each drum part separately first before putting it all together.

THIS LAND IS YOUR LAND

Words and Music by
Woody Guthrie

This land is your land, this land is my land from Cal - i -

for - nia to the New York is - lands; from the red - wood

for - ests to the gulf stream wat - er; this land was made for you and me.

THE HI-HAT CYMBALS

The **hi-hat cymbals** can be used instead of the ride cymbal. They are two cymbals on a stand activated by a pedal. Use the **hi-hat clutch** on the top cymbal to adjust the cymbals so they are about an inch apart. Using your right stick, hit the hi-hat on either the edge of the cymbals with the shoulder of the stick, or on the top surface with the tip of the stick. There are several ways to use the hi-hat foot pedal:

- Hold the pedal down tight with your left foot for a closed sound.

- Hold the pedal down not as tight for a loose, half-open sound.

- Lift your left foot all the way up for an open sound.

- You can also make a sound by just depressing the pedal to close the cymbals without hitting them at all with the stick.

Let's try a groove using your right stick on the **closed hi-hat**. Hold the hi-hat pedal down tightly for the closed sound.

TIPPING MY HAT

Repeat signs have two dots before or after a double bar line:

They simply tell you to repeat everything in between.

FREE FALLIN'

Words and Music by Tom Petty
and Jeff Lynne

After you learn the drum part to this next song, try singing along as you play.

ANOTHER ONE BITES THE DUST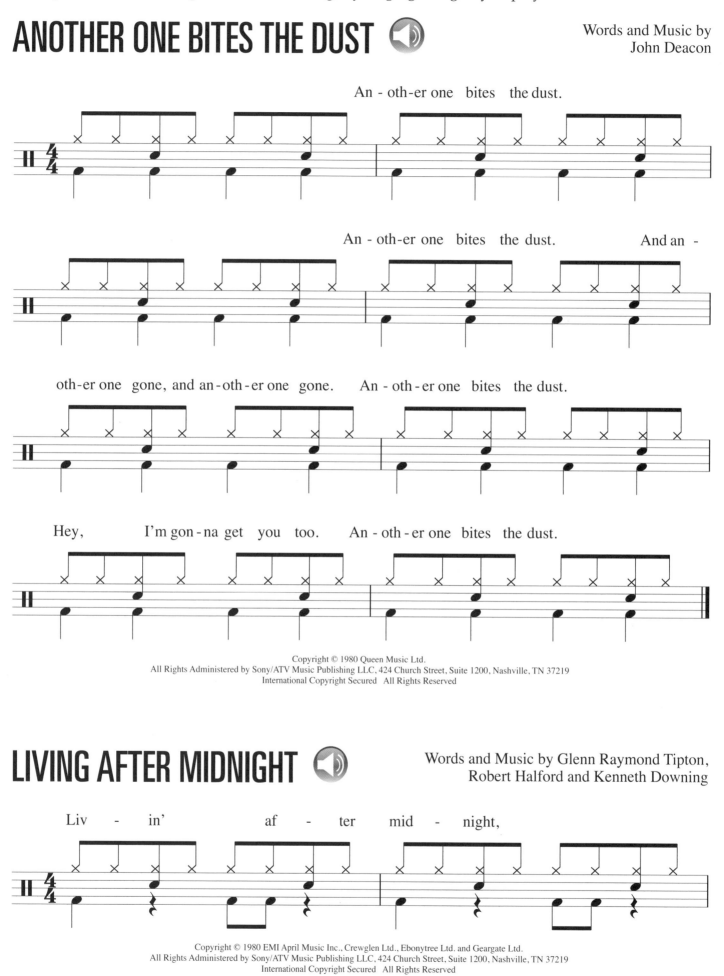

Words and Music by
John Deacon

An - oth-er one bites the dust.

An - oth-er one bites the dust. And an -

oth-er one gone, and an-oth-er one gone. An - oth-er one bites the dust.

Hey, I'm gon-na get you too. An - oth-er one bites the dust.

LIVING AFTER MIDNIGHT

Words and Music by Glenn Raymond Tipton,
Robert Halford and Kenneth Downing

Liv - in' af - ter mid - night,

rock - in'   to the dawn.

Lov - in'   till the morn - in',   then I'm gone.

I'm   gone.

If you release some pressure with your left foot on the hi-hat pedal and hit the cymbals with your stick, you'll create the **half-open hi-hat** sound. You'll know if you're doing it correctly if you hear the cymbals "sizzle" together. On the music staff, the half-open hi-hat is shown as an "ø" above each regular hi-hat note, like this:

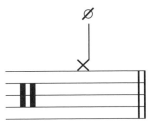

PETER GUNN 🔊

Theme Song from the Television Series
By Henry Mancini

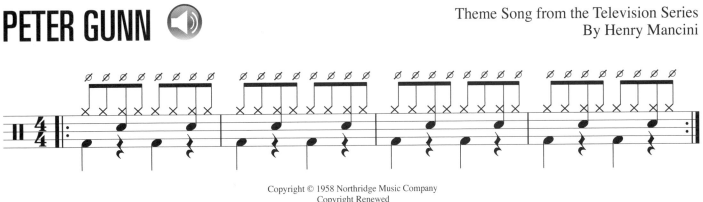

You can also play the hi-hat without sticks. By stepping on the pedal with your left foot, you can make the cymbals hit each other. This will be shown stem down just below the staff, in the same position as the bass drum, but with an "x" note.

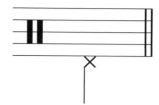

Rest your foot on the hi-hat pedal until you need to play it. Just lift your foot then press down the pedal to make the foot hi-hat sound. Hold it down (closed) until you need to play it again.

MY LEFT FOOT

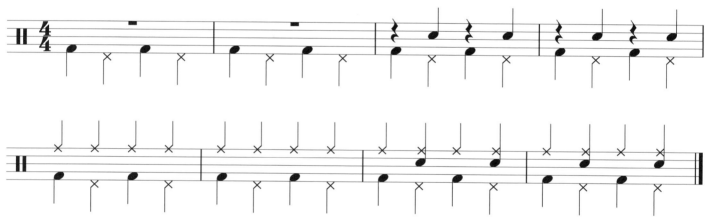

Using the **open hi-hat** sometimes can add cool variations to your grooves. An "o" above the hi-hat note tells you to play it open. Hit the hi-hat cymbals with your right stick like the half-open sound, but let the cymbals open completely with the foot pedal after you hit them. Notice the foot hi-hat telling you when to close the cymbals.

FAT HAT

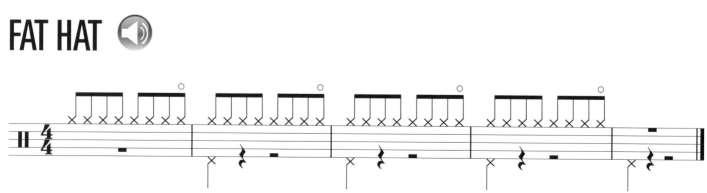

GRAND OPENING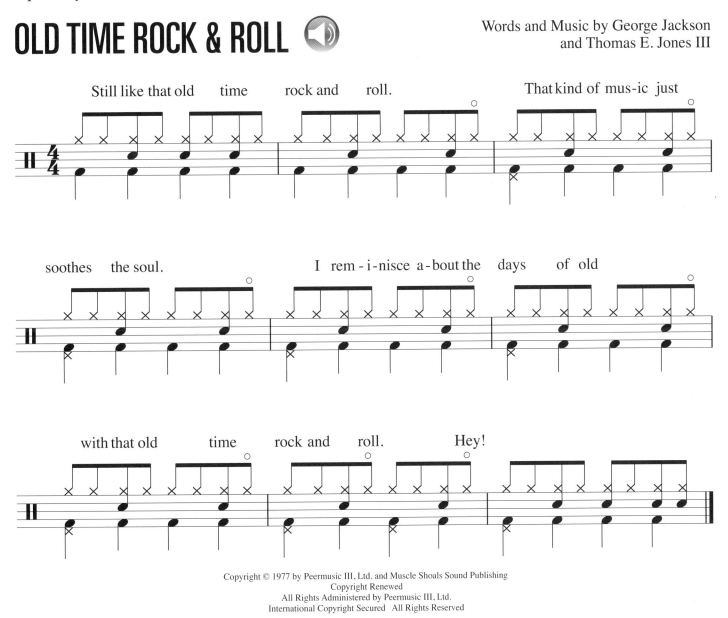

You will use both feet and both hands to play the groove in this classic song. Work out each part separately first and take it slow.

OLD TIME ROCK & ROLL

Words and Music by George Jackson
and Thomas E. Jones III

Still like that old time rock and roll. That kind of mus-ic just

soothes the soul. I rem - i -nisce a -bout the days of old

with that old time rock and roll. Hey!

THE CRASH CYMBAL

The **crash cymbal** is used to accent changes in the music and mark different sections of a song. You may have a separate crash cymbal, or just a combination crash/ride cymbal. For either one, you would hit the cymbal on the edge with the shoulder of the stick.

The crash cymbal is typically hit at the same time as the bass drum or snare drum. It is written on a line just above the staff called a **ledger line**.

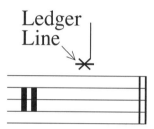

I CRASHED 🔊

SMASH AND CRASH 🔊

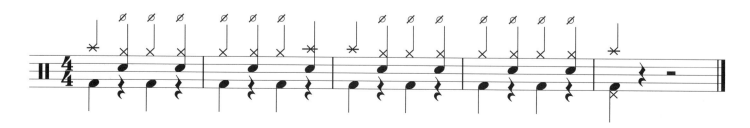

18

MORE NOTES AND RESTS

Sixteenth notes look like eighth notes but with a second flag added to the stem.

Two or more sixteenth notes are joined together with a double beam.

Count sixteenth notes as "1, e, and, a, 2, e, and, a," and so on. Get to know them with these snare drum exercises first, and count out loud as you play.

SIXTEENTH NOTES

Sixteenth rests have the same value as the sixteenth note, but are silent. Sixteenth rests look like an eighth rest on top of another eighth rest: ⅞

SIXTEENTH RESTS

Now try sixteenth notes in this full drumset example.

QUICK HAND

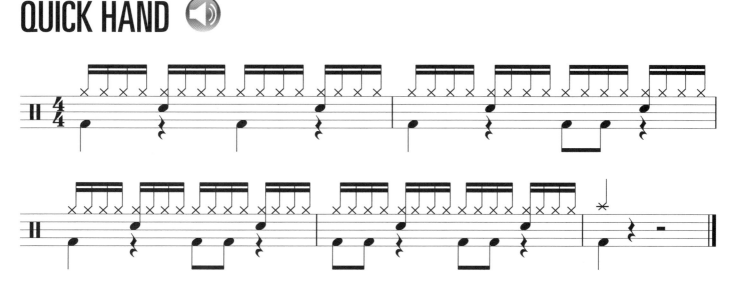

A **dot** (.) extends a note or rest by one-half of its value. For drummers, the two most common are the **dotted quarter** and **dotted eighth**.

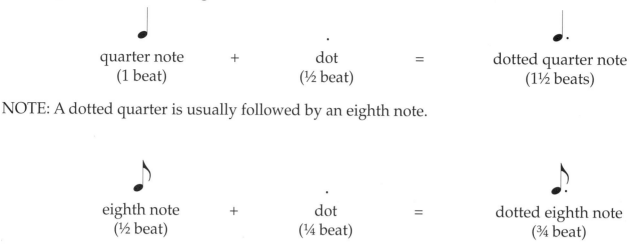

quarter note + dot = dotted quarter note
(1 beat)   (½ beat)   (1½ beats)

NOTE: A dotted quarter is usually followed by an eighth note.

eighth note + dot = dotted eighth note
(½ beat)   (¼ beat)   (¾ beat)

NOTE: A dotted eighth is usually connected to a sixteenth, like this:

Listen to the audio track for this next song to get a feel for the new dotted rhythm, then try playing it.

NEW KID IN TOWN

Words and Music by John David Souther,
Don Henley and Glenn Frey

WHEN THE LEVEE BREAKS

Words and Music by Jimmy Page, Robert Plant,
John Paul Jones, John Bonham
and Memphis Minnie

THE CROSS-STICK

Cross-stick (sometimes called **rim click** or **side stick**) is a popular sound used in many styles of music. To produce the cross-stick sound, flip the stick in your left hand around so that you are holding the shoulder of the stick. Lay the stick across the snare with the tip of the stick on the head, and the shaft closest to the butt end on the rim. Lift the stick up while keeping the tip on the snare head, and bring the butt end back down to hit the rim. You should hear a "click"-type sound.

On the staff, a circle around the snare note tells you it's to be played cross-stick.

STIR IT UP

Words and Music by
Bob Marley

THE TOM-TOMS

Tom-toms (or just **toms** for short) add tonal "color" to your sound. They are great for use in fills. A **fill** is a short break in the groove—a change that "fills in the gaps" of the music and/or signals the end of a phrase. It's kind of like a mini-solo. Your drumset may have two or more tom-toms. More toms give you more tonal variation, but two or three are typical. In this book we'll be using just two: high and low.

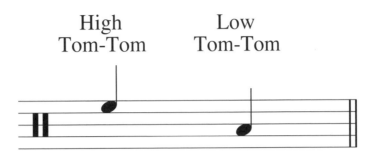

LOTS OF DRUMS

GROOVE AND FILL

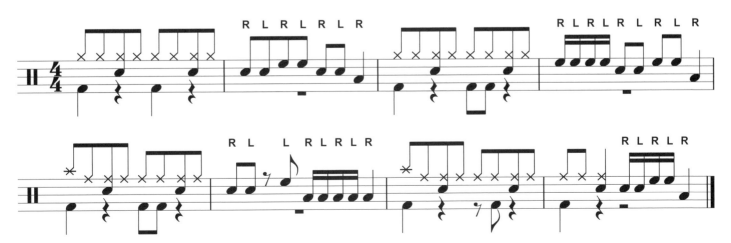

WILD THING

Words and Music by
Chip Taylor

GIMME SOME LOVIN'

Words and Music by Steve Winwood,
Muff Winwood and Spencer Davis

CRAZY TRAIN

Words and Music by Ozzy Osbourne,
Randy Rhoads and Bob Daisley

Sometimes a song may begin with several measures of rest for the drummer. A simple way to show multiple measures of rest would look like this:

In this case, it shows four measures of rest like in the beginning of the next song "Boulevard of Broken Dreams." You would count it like this: **1**, 2, 3, 4, **2**, 2, 3, 4, **3**, 2, 3, 4, **4**, 2, 3, 4.

BOULEVARD OF BROKEN DREAMS

Words by Billie Joe
Music by Green Day

Intro
Moderately slow ♩ = 84

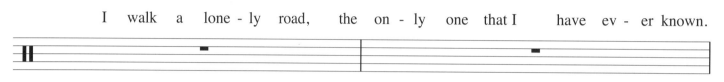

Verse

I walk a lone-ly road, the on-ly one that I have ev-er known.

Don't know where it goes, but it's home to me and I walk a-lone.

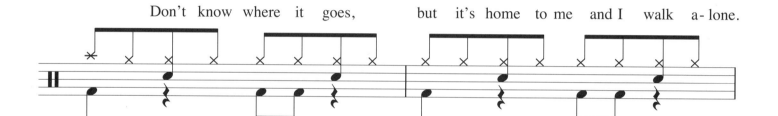

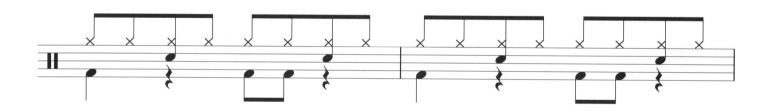

I walk this emp-ty street on the bou-le-vard of bro-ken dreams,

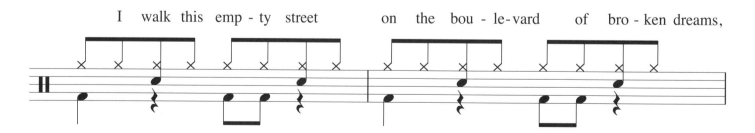

where the cit-y sleeps and I'm the on-ly one and I walk a-lone.

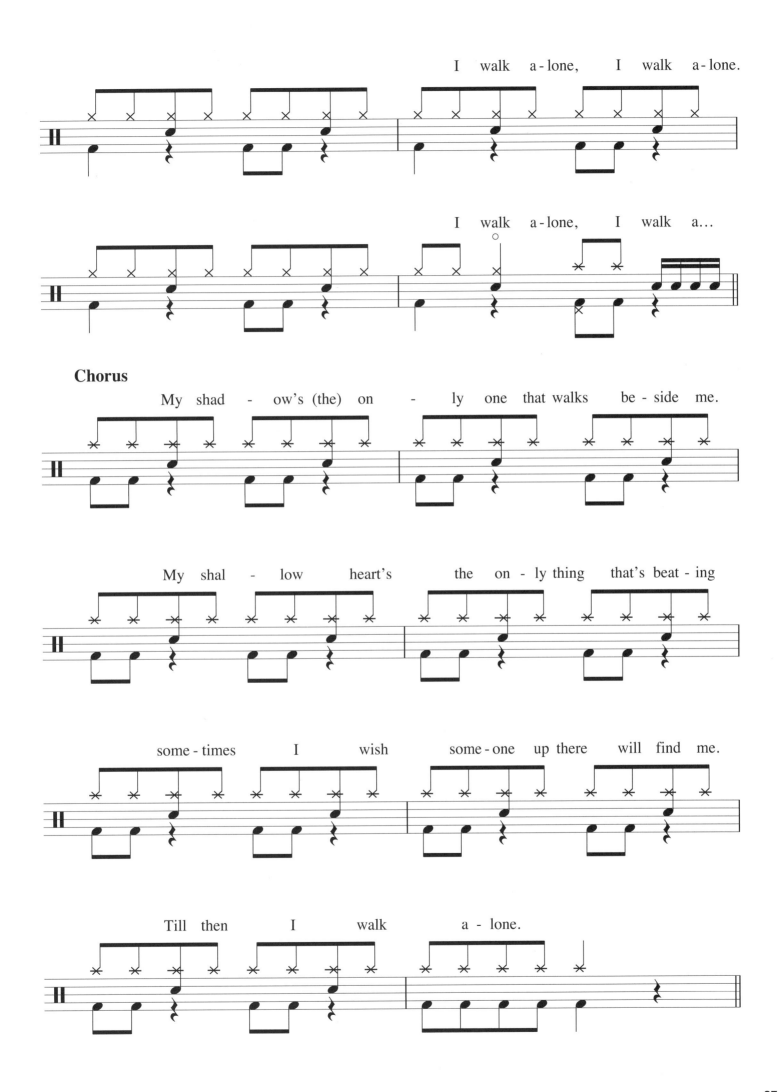

Chorus

Interlude

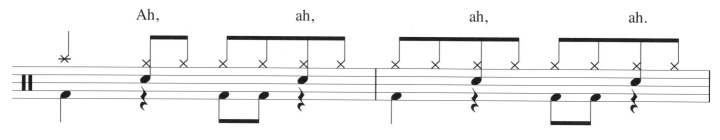

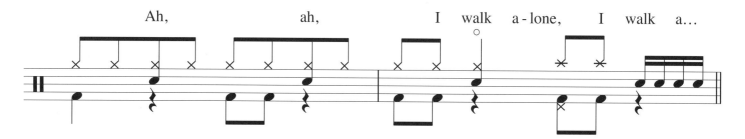

Guitar Solo

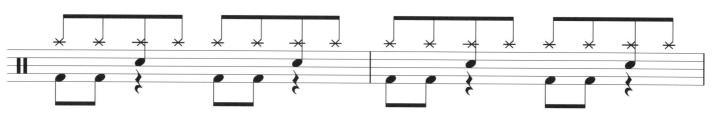

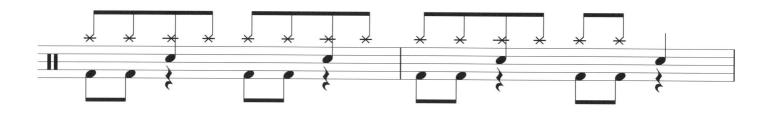

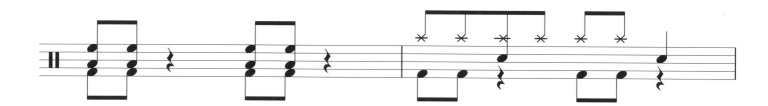

Verse

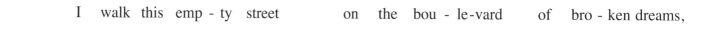

where the cit - y sleeps   and I'm the   on - ly one   and I   walk   a...

Chorus

My shad - ow's (the) on - ly one that walks be - side me.

My shal - low heart's   the on - ly thing   that's beat - ing.

Some - times   I   wish   some - one   up there   will   find me.

Till then   I   walk   a - lone.

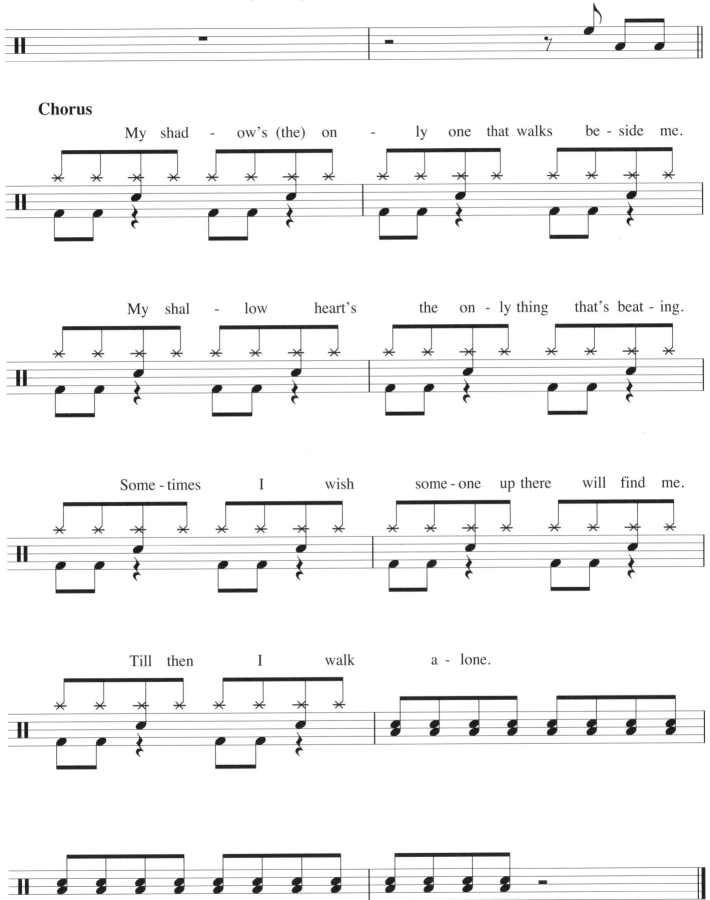

SURFIN' U.S.A.

Words and Music by
Chuck Berry

Verse
Moderately fast ♩ = 130

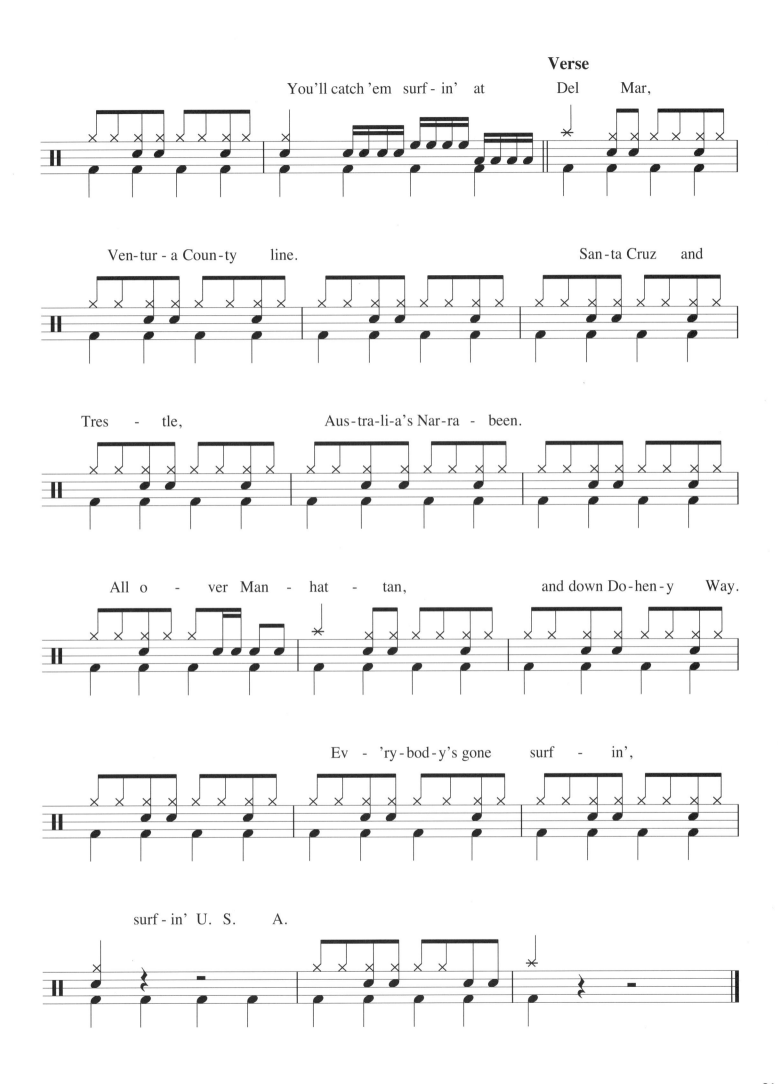

Verse

You'll catch 'em surf - in' at Del Mar,

Ven-tur - a Coun-ty line. San-ta Cruz and

Tres - tle, Aus-tra-li-a's Nar-ra - been.

All o - ver Man - hat - tan, and down Do-hen-y Way.

Ev - 'ry-bod-y's gone surf - in',

surf - in' U. S. A.

CERTIFICATE OF ACHIEVEMENT

Congratulations to

_____

(YOUR NAME)

_____

(DATE)

You have completed

DRUMS FOR KIDS

_____

(TEACHER SIGNATURE)